SAFE HAVEN
THE DEVOTIONAL

SAFE HAVEN
THE DEVOTIONAL

GREGORY A. SHUMAKE

XULON PRESS

Xulon Press
2301 Lucien Way #415
Maitland, FL 32751
407.339.4217
www.xulonpress.com

© 2022 by Gregory A. Shumake

All rights reserved solely by the author. The author guarantees all contents are original and do not infringe upon the legal rights of any other person or work. No part of this book may be reproduced in any form without the permission of the author.

Due to the changing nature of the Internet, if there are any web addresses, links, or URLs included in this manuscript, these may have been altered and may no longer be accessible. The views and opinions shared in this book belong solely to the author and do not necessarily reflect those of the publisher. The publisher therefore disclaims responsibility for the views or opinions expressed within the work.

Unless otherwise indicated Scripture quotations taken from the New King James Version (NKJV). Copyright © 1982 by Thomas Nelson, Inc. Used by permission. All rights reserved.

Paperback ISBN-13: 978-1-66285-111-7
Ebook ISBN-13: 978-1-66285-112-4

Table of Contents

Dedication vii
Preface. ix
Day 1 - "Waltz of Eden" - A Hunger for His Presence 1
Day 2 - "Each Time I Think of You" - You Fill Up My Senses 6
Day 3 - "Safe Haven" - The Place of Rest 11
Day 4 - "Hineini" - I'm Right Here 15
Day 5 - "Meditation" - Peace Perfected 20
Day 6 - "You Are My Hearts Desire" - Closeness 25
Day 7 - "The Longing of My Heart" - Show Me Your Face 30
Day 8 - "Amazing Grace" - Really Living. 35

Dedication:

To Brenda: Your tireless endeavor to make our home a "safe haven" does not go unnoticed. You are a jewel in the crown of the Lord. I hope I make you proud in all I do. "You raise me up so I can walk on mountains."

To The Rock Family Worship Center: You embody the mission statement "Love God, Love People." It is an honor and a privilege to serve the Lord by serving you.

To you, the reader: It is my prayer that, in some way, these words will be an encouragement to you and strength to your heart. May you find peace in the safe arms of the Lord each day.

PREFACE:

For as long as I can recall, I have had a deep desire for others to draw close to God and be free from all the things in their lives that keep Him at arm's length. I believe that, as Matt 12:34-35 states, "Out of the abundance of the heart, the mouth speaks," out of the abundance of the heart, the life will be lived. Yet many live their lives enduring each day and striving to work for God, hoping their work will establish the closeness with God they desire. I believe this is far from the truth. God wants people who press in daily to know Him, learn of Him, understand His heart even though they do not always understand His ways, and live their lives out of that reality.

Thus, this volume has been created.

I hope that as you read these humble attempts to help you in your intimacy with God, each one will serve as a catalyst for you to dig deeper into the Lover of your soul. This devotional also serves as a companion to my piano project of soft meditative piano music, also entitled "Safe Haven." Each entry here bears the song's name on the musical project, so you can go through them as you listen. I pray that as you walk through these pages, you will be able to see deeper into your own heart and His and that you and the Lord will meet with each other there. I pray that you will hear Him in such undeniable ways that your life will never be the same. Lastly, Michael Card, the fantastic songwriter, worshiper, musician, and speaker, wrote a song long ago entitled "Joy in the Journey." In that song, he makes the following statement:

> There is a joy in the journey
> There's a light we can love on the way

> There is a wonder and wildness to life
> And freedom for those who obey [1]

That's my desire for you. I desire you to discover the joy in your journey with God daily. He has amazing adventures for you if you press through the noise to hear His voice and follow Him. May you sense His deep, all-encompassing love for you each day as you walk through these simple pages.

> "The Lord bless you and keep you. The Lord make His face to shine upon you. The Lord lift His countenance upon you, and give you His peace." (Num 6:24-26)

---

[1] (1) From the album "The Final Word" Copyright: ℗© 1987 Sparrow Records

—GREGORY A. SHUMAKEL

Day 1 - "Waltz of Eden" - A Hunger for His Presence

You know, there has been much mentioned in recent days about the presence of God. It seems to be the hot topic of most anything about worship. One could even begin to take the subject for granted because of this, but I pray we never do. All of humanity truly hungers for the presence of God. In reality, nothing else will ever truly satisfy, but rather only offer a temporary numbing to true hunger in our hearts. This hunger is at the bedrock of our lives as people, but many are unaware of it. For example, Paul the apostle ran into this dynamic in Acts 17. His spirit was grieved when he saw the extent of idol worship the Athenians exhibited. It was evidently over the top and to an extreme. They had gods for virtually everything under heaven because they didn't want to offend any. And just in case they missed any of their gods, they had even set up an altar to "The Unknown God." Paul, seizing the opportunity, continued to describe who this unknown God is to them. Some believed, and others sneered and mocked. But light shined in darkness in the hearts of some, and they were added to the Kingdom of God.

In contrast, the Psalmist David in Psalm 63 expresses the longing of the heart of a true worshiper. This heart longs desperately for the Lord and his presence. The main focus of this psalm is the cry of the worshiper for the presence of his God. He was enthralled with God, yearning even in his flesh to be with Him. His satisfaction came from the presence of the Lord, and his mouth was filled with praise unto God. The heart that pangs of hunger for the Living God exemplifies this reality: the only satisfaction for my entire being is God and God alone.

Even today, we hunger for the presence of God. That's what the Athenians truly craved, and that's what the Psalmist displayed in his discourse. The difference is that one was a FOCUSED HUNGER while the other was a MISGUIDED HUNGER. The Athenians didn't know that it was the Lord God Almighty that they desired. They knew that someone or something else out there needed to be worshiped. Notice that those who believed in Paul's message put away all other gods to serve and worship the One True God alone. David made his declaration and focus clear; there is no other god but the Lord God. Only He could "satisfy his soul with marrow and fatness," and as a result, his mouth would praise God "with joyful lips."

What about you? What is the focus of your heart? Have the struggles of life caused you to wander into escape mode instead of retaining confidence in the living God to empower you to overcome them? That was the heart of the Psalmist, and so it can be for you. He became empowered to overcome by the presence of the Living God. He knew that he would be transformed as he spent time with Him, even if his circumstances weren't. He knew his perspective of life would change if he could only behold the face of his Lord. That is available to you today and every day, for the arms and heart of the Father are open to you continually. His invitation still stands. There is a hunger in your heart that will ONLY be satisfied with Him and Him alone. Don't delay, but instead, enter in TODAY! He loves you and welcomes you.

> "Father, thank you for this day that You have given and for Your ever-abiding presence. I welcome You on this day and ask that You help me recognize Your presence around me and within me. I set my heart upon You in all things today and agree with You for Your will to be done in me. I choose to have a heart of praise toward You this day. Thank You for Your loving embrace. In Jesus' name, Amen."

Scripture Passages:

Psalm 63:1-8
Psalm 42:1-8

Thoughts to Ponder:

What are some of the things that fill your attention? What do you find yourself dwelling on the most in life?

As you consider these things, examine what they produce in your life. Do they cause you to desire God more? Do they bring confidence toward the Lord as in Psalm 63?

Consider what you can do to cultivate a hunger more of God's presence in your life.

Notes:

Day 2 - "Each Time I Think of You"- You Fill Up My Senses

One Christmas season, I was in a Famous Footwear store where my daughter, Mia (pronounced My-yuh), once worked. I had come in to drop off lunch for her. She took me for a little stroll around the store to show me some of the shoes there. She then showed me a pair of shoes she had set aside. I was thrilled and filled with anticipation. Then my eyes fell upon another pair of shoes I'd always wanted but could never seem to afford. "Oh, I love these shoes!" I said. "I've always wanted a pair of these. I think they're so cool." "Maybe in a little while, Dad," Mia said, which I totally understood.

Then came Christmas. We were all there unwrapping gifts and had finished, so I thought, because out came one last gift from my daughter. I opened it, and to my amazement, there was the pair of shoes I'd wanted! I was aghast, and I thanked her repeatedly with tears streaming down my face. I was not expecting such a gift.

You may say, "You were crying over a pair of shoes?" No, not just over the shoes, but that my daughter had me on her mind and thought of blessing me with something I always wanted. This is such a little thing to some, but it was enormous to me.

Similarly, that's how God is toward you. He thinks of you often, more often than you could ever imagine. He knows your needs and what would best fit you and your life. He cares about everything that touches you and is concerned about every area of your life, right down to the number of hairs on your head. He loves you deeply, and because of that love, He walks with you closer than a brother, has made His abode within you, yearns to lead and guide you day and night, and yearns to fellowship with you constantly. He wants to take walks with you, talk, laugh and cry with you. Like my daughter did with me in that store, God wants to do with you. He has so much He wants to show you of His Kingdom and His plan for your life. And sometimes, He wants to bless you just to see the smile and joy it brings your way. He has made provision for you to come into His presence wherein He welcomes you with open arms of everlasting love. Like the John Denver song, "You Fill Up My Senses," know that you sincerely do fill the senses of your Heavenly Father.

So as you start your day today, begin with the reception of that love from Him. He offers you a daily invitation to meet together, so take Him at His word. Let Him love on you today before you face anything else. His love will cover you constantly as you acknowledge Him. Draw close to Him today. As you read these lyrics from John Denver, hear them from the heart of God to you:

> "You fill up my senses like a night in the forest,
> like the mountains in springtime, like a walk in the rain,
> like a storm in the desert, like a sleepy blue ocean.
> You fill up my senses. Come fill me again.
>
> Come let me love you, let me give my life to you,
> let me drown in your laughter, let me live-(*my edit*) in your arms,
> let me lay down beside you, let me always be with you.
> Come let me love you, come love me again."
>
> John Denver

"Father, I love You and thank You for loving me. Today, I set my heart to receive Your love, and even as I extend my love and adoration to You. I choose to count You faithful and trustworthy toward me, and I will be faithful to You by Your grace. Thank You for going before me today and making my path straight as I press on to keep my mind set on You. I receive Your grace for this day, and I put my trust in You." In Jesus' name, Amen.

Scripture Passages:

Jer 29:11-14
Psalm 40:5-8, 17

Thoughts to Ponder:

It's easy to love on God, but how easy is it for you to receive His love toward you?

Are there any hindrances in you that keep you at arm's length from the love of God?

What are you willing to do to see those hindrances removed, freeing you to receive the love of God fully in your life?

Notes:

Day 3 - "Safe Haven" - The Place of Rest

What pictures come to mind when you hear the word "fortress?" Do you think of an impenetrable edifice that no amount of firepower could break through? Do you picture high walls several feet thick? How about the word "Sanctuary?" Centuries ago, people fleeing enemies would run to the church for sanctuary, which was considered safe and holy ground where no harm could be done. The occupants therein were safe from all attacks as long as they stayed within its walls. It was considered a "safe place."

I'm reminded of the day I asked my in-laws for my wife's hand in marriage. My Father-in-law, Gary, asked me what we would do about kids. This was a concern of his because we are an interracially married couple. I remember my response. I said, "I believe that if we make our home a safe place for our kids and deal with the world's influences, we'll be ok. It will not be flawless, but there is a greater chance of succeeding with them as long as they know that home is a safe place." Our children are adults now and are doing well overall. It was not that we were such great parents by any means! We simply tried to instill in them a more positive reality than their surroundings to the best of our ability. We wanted to make it where they could bring all the things they have gone through in their days to the home, and we'd deal with them according to the wisdom of the Lord and to the insight gained just by living life. Some of the things they'd bring home to discuss were intense, but God gave wisdom to share. Sometimes they listened to the wisdom the Lord gave us. Sometimes they didn't. Sometimes we listened to God's wisdom, and sometimes we missed it, but the understanding was there nonetheless. They knew that they could be themselves at home. They had to follow specific guidelines and standards while at home, but at least they could come to a place where the issues they'd just gotten out of wouldn't have any authority or power.

Similarly, the presence of the Lord is like that. Coming home to meet with the Lord is the safest place you could ever be. Nothing can touch you when you are engulfed in His presence. It is where you can just be yourself and not worry about being attacked by the same things that weighed you down. It's the place where weights are removed, pressures are eased, joy is restored, peace is experienced, and there is a standard of conduct in His presence that you will reap the benefits of if you abide by them.

On this day, take some time to "retreat" into His presence and find rest from the hustle and bustle of everyday living to gain heaven's perspective. When you see through heaven's eyes, your world has more significant potential to look better than it would if you looked through your own. Find HIS joy, HIS peace, HIS love toward you, and let Him minister to YOU there in that secret place.

> "Father, today I choose to rest in You, knowing that whatever I face today, You have already overcome. Therefore I can rejoice and be glad because You have made provision for me to be at peace at all times. Lord, I choose to be close to You today. In Jesus' name, Amen.

Scripture Passages:

Psalm 144
Psalm 125
Proverbs 18:10

Thoughts to Ponder:

It's easy to love on God, but how easy is it for you to receive His love toward you?

Are there any hindrances in you that keep you at arm's length from the love of God?

What are you willing to do to see those hindrances removed, freeing you to receive the love of God fully in your life?

Notes:

Day 4 - "Hineini" - I'm Right Here

Dry times. Everyone goes through them. In Isaiah's day, he lived among a dry people. He lived among people who were considered unclean and far away from God. Then, one day, he came face to face with the Holy One and came face to face with his own state of being. He describes what he saw, seeing the Lord "sitting on a throne high and lifted up, and the train of His robe filled the temple." This was a regal sight, one of infinite royalty and splendor. Majestic beings called Seraphim circled the throne, crying out, "Holy, holy, holy is the Lord of Hosts; the whole earth is full of His glory!" This cry was so spectacular that the doorposts were shaken, and the house was filled with smoke. At that moment, in the presence of someone so incredibly holy and perfect, he had no other recourse but to acknowledge the truth of his situation, "Woe is me, for I am undone! Because I am a man of unclean lips, and I dwell in the midst of a people of unclean lips; For my eyes have seen the King, the Lord of Hosts" (verses 1-5).

Then something strange happened. One of the heavenly beings, the seraphim that flew above the throne of God, flew to Isaiah with a live coal taken from the altar with tongs and touched his lips with it. Then the seraphim declared that Isaiah's uncleanness was purged and his sins were removed. And lastly, there was an invitation to go and stand for the Lord. Isaiah responded, "Hineini!" meaning, "Here am I, Lord! I'll go for You! Send me!"

Hineini (pronounced HEE-NAY-NEE) is an interesting word, but it means much more than a simple reply of here I am. The actual meaning is, "Here am I. ALL that I have is yours. ALL that I am is yours. ALL my resources are available to you at all times WITHOUT reservation." It creates quite a different picture, right? This is what Isaiah was saying in response to the voice of the Lord.

Notice that the seraphim flew to HIM as soon as Isaiah confessed the truth of how was. He didn't have to come groveling on his hands and knees, declaring, "Unclean! Unclean! I'm so worthless and pathetic! I don't know why You'd ever want me, Lord, but if You can do something with this horrible piece of useless flesh, here I am!" No, not at all. God didn't even give him a chance to go there. Instead, the seraphim flew to him to take care of what stood in the way. God desired to use Isaiah for the purposes of the Kingdom, purposes that he was created for from the beginning!

There is another amazing side of Hineini that you need to know. In Isaiah 58:9, after describing the type of fast God has chosen, a true fast, God says an incredible thing: "Then you shall call, and the Lord will answer; You shall cry, and He will say, 'Here I am!'" This is the same word Isaiah responded to God with. "Here am I. ALL that I have is yours. ALL that I am is yours. ALL my resources are available to you at all times WITHOUT reservation."

As you begin your day today, recognize that God has made Himself utterly available to you more than you could ever imagine. If there is anything that stands in the way of your intimacy with Him, He has made provision for that as well. There is an old saying that "God is just a prayer away." That is the truth, my Friend. Give everything over to Him today first and foremost, and He will take care of all the rest. He will fly to you as the seraphim did to Isaiah without giving him a chance to entertain the possibility of rejection, for there is no rejection in God toward His children. He will purge whatever the issue is and immediately beckon you to come closer and fellowship with Him. You will hear Him say...." HINEINI!"

> "Father, Thank You for making Yourself and all that You have available to me in Jesus today. I choose to follow You, Lord, and make all that I am and all that I have available to You. Use me as You desire, Father. I choose to draw close to You. I am Yours."

Scripture Passages:

Jeremiah 31:3
Isaiah 54:4-17

Thoughts to Ponder:

How willing are you to surrender to God in consideration of the meaning of Hineini?

When you realize God Himself says "Hineini" to you, what thoughts come to mind?

In what areas do you see the need to surrender to God in order to experience the effect of Hineini in your life?

Notes:

Day 5 - "Meditation" - Peace Perfected

The gentle breeze. A new sunrise. Green grass and the sounds of the open meadow. The bubbling brook flows delicately over the small rocks and pebbles. There is peace. This is a scene that is available to us at all times in the presence of the Almighty. We all go through so many different things and life that weigh us down, But the Lord calls us to dwell in a place where we remain steadfast and secure in His love and presence. He goes to great extremes to keep us in this place if we would only allow Him to.

Scripture says, "In the presence of the Lord there is fullness of joy, and at Your right hand are pleasures forevermore (Ps 16:11)." This is the case always, no matter the circumstance. Have you ever been in the midst of a place where things are going haywire all around you? The stress of life and responsibility tug and pull on you so tightly that you feel as if you are about to lose your footing. The weight of the world seems to rest solely on your shoulders. Pressure to survive, make decisions, fix issues, and provide hit you hard. Yet, the Lord offers His presence to calm and sustain you in this place.

Consider Jesus in the boat on the water amid the storm. The waves were beating upon the boat and coming into it. The disciples were engulfed in fear for their very lives. This was a difficult situation, yet Jesus was asleep in the midst of their struggle. They cried out to Him, asking if He even cared that they were "perishing." Ever been there? Have you ever felt like you were sinking and began to wonder if you were all alone or that even Jesus had forsaken you? Yet Jesus stood and rebuked the wind and the waves, and all became calm. Then He turned to His disciples and said, "Why did you doubt?". He had promised they would get to the other side, and He never breaks His promises, no matter what came their way. Jesus is the "prototype" for us in living for God because that is precisely what He did all His earthly life. He said, "Peace I leave to you; MY peace I give you, not as the world gives, give I to you." The peace Jesus walked in was an all-encompassing peace fueled by faith and ultimate confidence in the Father. He never worried. Even in the garden, when He prayed for the Father to let the cup of suffering He was about to partake of, He wasn't concerned. Instead, He was anticipating the insurmountable pain He was about to endure.

I submit to you that the same is available to you today. His peace is yours at any given moment, and the enemy would want to take your focus off of this promise. If he can get you to focus on the things of life over the promises of God, he will begin to direct your day and your life. I encourage you to stand firm in the Lord today, allowing Him to empower you to stand. No matter what you may face today, God has made promises to you regarding your life. Come what may, He WILL keep His promise and will cause you to grow in the midst of it. He will solidify His word to you during the storm or the struggle, and your faith and confidence will grow deeper in Him. This is a certainty. Be encouraged. Peaceful waters are available to you in the midst of any storm. Provision is yours amid any lack. Restoration of hope is provided for you whenever you require it, and He will cause even those things that come against you not to affect your heart as you yield to Him. Receive that today and go in the power of the Spirit.

> "Father, today I receive Your peace and restoration. I permit You to order my steps today and guide me into Your rest even during turmoil. Lord, I declare that I trust You completely today and receive Your power to walk in the power of Your Holy Spirit. In Jesus Name, Amen."

Scripture Passages:

Isaiah 55:11-13
John 14:27
Isaiah 26:3-4

Thoughts to Ponder:

What are some things that can take away your peace?

What ways can you think of to maintain and guard the peace God gives?

Notes:

Day 6 -
"You Are My Hearts Desire" -
Closeness

You know, I've always been amazed at the discourse that took place in the upper room during the Passover observance Jesus had with His disciples before the sacrifice of His life. It is both intriguing and inviting. I am referencing John 13:23-26. Here, John the apostle was at the supper with the rest. Still, something was different regarding his interaction with Jesus and the others' interaction. He wasn't reclining like the other disciples. Instead, he was leaning on the chest of Jesus. What a picture. He had such a love for the Savior that being close to Him was of the utmost importance. Take a moment and recall the discourse. There they all are relaxing and reclining around the table, and out of nowhere, Jesus says someone would betray Him. All the other disciples questioned Him about who it was, but Jesus never told them specifically. Imagine how perplexing that had to be. This Savior in Whom the disciples placed their trust is saying that one of them was to betray Him but concealed the person's identity. Then Peter motions to John to ask Him because John was closest to Jesus. Notice what John did: he leaned back onto Jesus and asked Him who it was. At this, Jesus, without revealing the name of the person, tells him that it's the one to whom He gives the bread after He dipped it. The word says that after He said this, He dipped the bread and gave it to Judas and does not state that any time had gone by before handing it to him. After doing so, Jesus tells Judas, "Hurry up and get it over with. [my paraphrase]" and it says that no one knew why Jesus said this to him. I submit to you that John knew because the actions Jesus did were in response to the question John had asked.

How does this apply to you? Again, good question. It applies because it has EVERYTHING to do with your relationship with God. It gives us an intimate picture of a passionate heart for the Savior. We see it in John. He cultivated a closer relationship with Jesus than any of the other disciples, and we are called to do the same. Life requires closeness. Life requires intimacy. Life requires transparency. And life requires total abandonment to the Lord as we walk with Him. This is what John shows us in the passage. Daniel 11:32 says, "...the people who KNOW their God will be strong and will do great exploits." The people who are close to the heart of God, hearing and feeling His heartbeat, will be strong, mighty, and effective. Notice also that as John stayed close to Jesus, he could hear and understand what no one else in the room understood or knew. I believe he knew who the betrayer was, but only because of closeness.

What do you need to hear from the heart of the Father today? What answers to questions do you need from the Spirit of the Living God? As you strive to live with Him in intimacy, transparency, total abandonment, and closeness, the Father will speak to you and show you "great and mighty things that you do not know – Jer. 33:3." John dared to be vulnerable to the Lord because he knew he could trust Him. How about you? Will you be willing to be susceptible to the love of God today? He has such beautiful things to share with you. It's an incredible adventure. So come and go for a ride. He invites you today. He's as close as a whisper.

> "Father, thank You for this day. Thank you for never leaving or forsaking me. Today, I will strive to walk closer to You, listening intently for Your voice with expectancy, knowing that You are faithful to keep your

promises. I place my complete trust in You. In Jesus' name, Amen."

Scripture Passages:

John 15:1-17
Psalm 25:1-15
John 13:23-26

Thoughts to Ponder:

Think back to when you first began your new life in Jesus. How was it?

As you look over your life, what things can you identify that may have moved you away from your closeness with the Lord?

Take some time to ask the Lord if there is anything in your life that is causing distance between you and His presence. Are you willing to surrender them to Him as He pinpoints them?

Notes:

Day 7 -
"The Longing of My Heart" -
Show Me Your Face

I love the presence of the Lord. When He shows up in the midst of worship, wild things happen. People can be healed, lives can be forever changed, and destinies can be discovered. On and on, the list can go. We often cry out for the Lord to show up in our midst because we have a need. I want to echo the cry of Moses' heart when he was with the Lord on the mountain, as expressed in the song written by Psalmist Don Potter, "Show Me Your Face." Moses' cry was the voice of one who had grown past seeing what His God could do. He had seen the pillar of fire and the cloud. He had seen the parting of the Red Sea. He had witnessed the feeding of the people with the quail and manna, but he was hungry to see the face of God. He wanted to experience God more intimately than ever before, but there was a problem. No man could see God's face and live. Therefore, since Moses could not see God's face, God permitted him to see all of His goodness. He set him in a prepared place on the mountain and revealed His goodness to Moses. Then we meet up with Jesus in John 14, where He says that He goes, "to prepare a place for you...that where I am, you may be also. (vs. 3)"

In reality, this is the cry of God's heart toward you. You yearn to be in God's presence and know Him more intimately as Moses desired, but what we often do not realize is that God desires for you to show yourself to Him as transparently as you desire Him to reveal Himself to you. Just as God prepared a place on the mountain for Moses to see God's goodness, Jesus has gone to prepare a place for you so that you can see

God's face. We can experience the presence of God like Moses did on the mountain, and one of the ways we can is in our worship.

Psalm 100 gives us the pattern to experience the presence of the Lord. It reads:

Make a joyful shout to the Lord all you lands! 2. Serve the Lord with gladness; come before His presence with singing. 3. KNOW that the Lord, HE IS GOD; It is He who has made us, and not we ourselves; We are His people and the sheep of His pasture. 4. Enter into His gates with thanksgiving and into His courts with praise. Be thankful unto Him and bless His name. 5. For the Lord is good; His mercy is everlasting, and His truth endures to all generations."

Did you notice verse 4? Praise and thanksgiving are the hinges upon which the doorway to His presence swings. It is based upon an understanding of who we are worshiping, hence the word "know" in verse 3. We are to KNOW, understand, and become totally convinced of the person of the Lord we worship. That knowledge and understanding undergird the worship we offer the Lord. As a result of knowledge of the rule and reign of God, His handiwork, and our position with Him, it gives birth to thanksgiving and praise. And as we do this from a heart of pure sincerity, His presence is free to manifest in the most miraculous ways.

Hosea 6:3 encourages us to "pursue the knowledge of the Lord." In this verse, the word "know" is the Hebrew word "YADA," which is the same word used in Genesis regarding Adam knowing Eve. It is ultimate transparency, nothing hidden, nothing withheld, complete and total trust. This is what you are asking for from the Lord, and it is indeed what He is asking for from you.

God wants to love on His children. He wants to love on you. He wants you to experience all that He has for you, as much as you are able to bear. He manifests Himself to you bit by bit, constantly growing you deeper and deeper into the understanding of who you are in Him and who He is in you. Worship causes an even more free exchange between you and God. Still, the ones who hunger for Who He is over WHAT He can do will walk away most fulfilled as a result of His presence. He will meet you at the point of your worship. Worship Him, Friend. If you praise Him simply because He is God, you will see Him manifest Himself to you in ways you couldn't have imagined.

> "Father, I love You. Thank You for loving me. I desire to know You more and more each day, so today, I set my heart to pursue You. In turn, I give myself totally and fully to You. I will do so without reservation because You are trustworthy and faithful. Thank You for Your presence with me now. In Jesus' name, Amen."

Scripture Passages:

Ex. 33:12-23
John 14:1-15

Thoughts to Ponder:

Is your worship of God more religion-based or relationship-based? (Is your worship dictated by what you should/shouldn't do, can/cannot say, etc.?)

What would you say is the difference between decency/order and freedom/liberty in worship?

In what ways can you strike a balance between the two?

Notes:

Day 8 - "Amazing Grace" - Really Living

When we think of grace, we often end at it simply meaning "unmerited favor." This is an accurate assessment of the word, for sure. We think of Ephesians 2:8 and how we were saved by grace. However, grace is much, much more.

Grace can be defined as "...deliverance from enemies, affliction, or adversity. It also denotes enablement, daily guidance, forgiveness, and preservation" - (http://www.allaboutgod.com/definition-of-gods-grace-faq.htm). Grace is something that goes beyond salvation into our daily existence. In His sovereign choosing, salvation is something that God provided for each of us, and we can reap its benefits by receiving Jesus as Lord. He then seals us with His Holy Spirit once we have believed (Eph. 1:13/4:30). Grace is applied in other areas of life as needed. God's power is perfected in weakness by grace (2 Cor. 12:9). The ability to be effective and productive, not just in the work of the Kingdom but in life, comes by the grace of God (1 Cor 15:10). We are filled with thanksgiving, which abounds to the glory of God because of grace (2 Cor 4:15), and we are accepted in the Beloved by the grace of God (Eph 1:6).

The grace of God empowers us to become who we are ordained to become and live the abundant life we were destined to live. It is one of heaven's greatest forces, yet this grace is both intricate and simplistic. We have seen its intricacy, but do we recognize its simplicity?

I'm reminded of my dear Friend Paul Wilbur when we would travel the world leading in and teaching on worship. Our travels were extensive, equalling about 280 days out of the year. We would go from airport to airport, hotel to hotel, venue to venue, and back home again. One day I asked him how he keeps up such a hectic schedule, to which he replied, "There's a grace for it. When the grace for this kind of travel lifts, it's time to make changes." I never forgot that simple reply. He was signifying that grace was not just available for the big things, but for something as simple as the ability to sit on a plane and travel for hours on end, and then pour out of your spirit to minister life to the nations.

Scripture records many that had the grace to stand in the face of adversaries, speak with boldness, love powerfully, and endure hardships with joy. The list of what grace supplies is endless. This is one of the reasons grace is so amazing. Because of His abundant amazing grace, we can experience so much more than we would without it.

As you begin your day today, recognize the grace of God available to you and take advantage of it. Lay claim to that grace and put it into action. God loves you too much to see you face each day without the ability to succeed. Are you anticipating challenges today? There's a grace to get through it. Are there stresses awaiting you? There's a grace to stand in it. Are you in the midst of an intense struggle? There's a grace to endure through it to the other side of it, and there is grace available for you, enabling you to receive His love for you right now, TODAY.

> "Father, today I receive Your grace for my life. Because of Your grace, I believe that I can do all things through Jesus, Who strengthens me. Thank you for enabling me to acknowledge You in all I do today and for guiding me and filling me with Your peace. I receive it all today, Lord, right now. In Jesus' name, Amen."

Scripture Passages:

Psalm 45:1-8
Proverbs 4:1-9
Jeremiah 31:1-14

Thoughts to Ponder:

Considering this brief study, in what ways have you seen the grace of God at work in your life?

What would you say is your responsibility regarding experiencing the grace of God in your life today and extending that grace to others?

Would you say there are limits to the grace of God? If so, what are they and why?

Notes:

CPSIA information can be obtained
at www.ICGtesting.com
Printed in the USA
BVHW071239020822
643617BV00006B/193